I Used to Play Piano

80s and 90s HITS

Arranged by Carol Matz

Foreword

The *I Used to Play Piano* series was designed for adults who have studied piano before and want to play again. The *I Used to Play Piano Refresher Course Book* (#22166) includes classical pieces, jazz and ragtime, etudes, pieces by well-known contemporary composers, traditional familiar favorites, as well as instructional text about playing piano.

Now adults will have a blast playing pop favorites in the correlating book, *I Used to Play Piano: 80s and 90s Hits.* Like the *Refresher Course Book,* this hits book is organized into units, progressing gradually from elementary through late intermediate in difficulty. Familiar pieces from recordings, Broadway, movies and television are included to study simultaneously with each corresponding unit in the *Refresher Course Book.*

Through this series, adults will be inspired to rediscover the joy of playing piano with the pop music they love.

ISBN-10: 0-7390-5589-5
ISBN-13: 978-0-7390-5589-2

Table of Contents

Unit One

Belinda Carlisle, lead singer of the all-female band The Go-Go's, struck out on her own in 1985 to pursue a solo singing career. "Heaven Is a Place on Earth," released in 1987, was her biggest hit, reaching #1 on the Billboard Hot 100 chart. Academy Award-winning actress Diane Keaton directed the music video for the song.

HEAVEN IS A PLACE ON EARTH

Words and Music by
Rick Nowels and Ellen Shipley
Arranged by Carol Matz

San Francisco-based rock band Journey recorded this smash hit in 1982 for their biggest-selling album entitled *Escape*. "Open Arms" earned the top spot on VH1's "25 Greatest Power Ballads" list, and was later recorded by Mariah Carey in 1996 for her album *Daydream*. In 2004, *American Idol* singers Clay Aiken and Kelly Clarkson featured the ever-popular song as a duet in their joint concert tour.

OPEN ARMS

Words and Music by
Jonathan Cain and Steve Perry
Arranged by Carol Matz

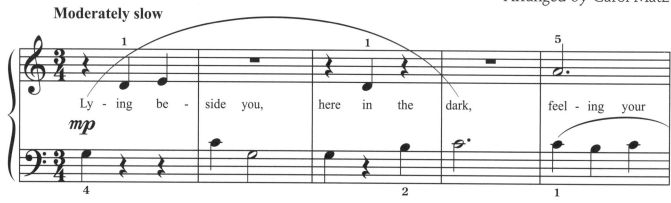

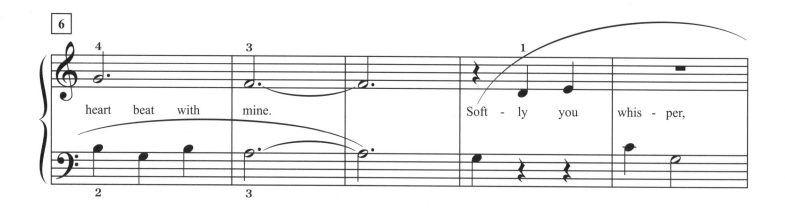

Unit Two

"I'll Be There for You," the upbeat theme song from the NBC sitcom *Friends,* was first recorded by the pop band The Rembrandts in 1994. The theme song became well known and loved by viewers, as *Friends* enjoyed a 10-year run and earned numerous awards, including six Emmy Awards and two Golden Globes.

I'LL BE THERE FOR YOU
(Theme from *Friends*)

Words by David Crane, Marta Kauffman,
Allee Willis, Phil Solem and Danny Wilde
Music by Michael Skloff
Arranged by Carol Matz

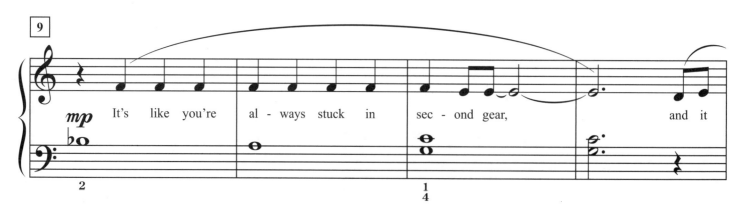

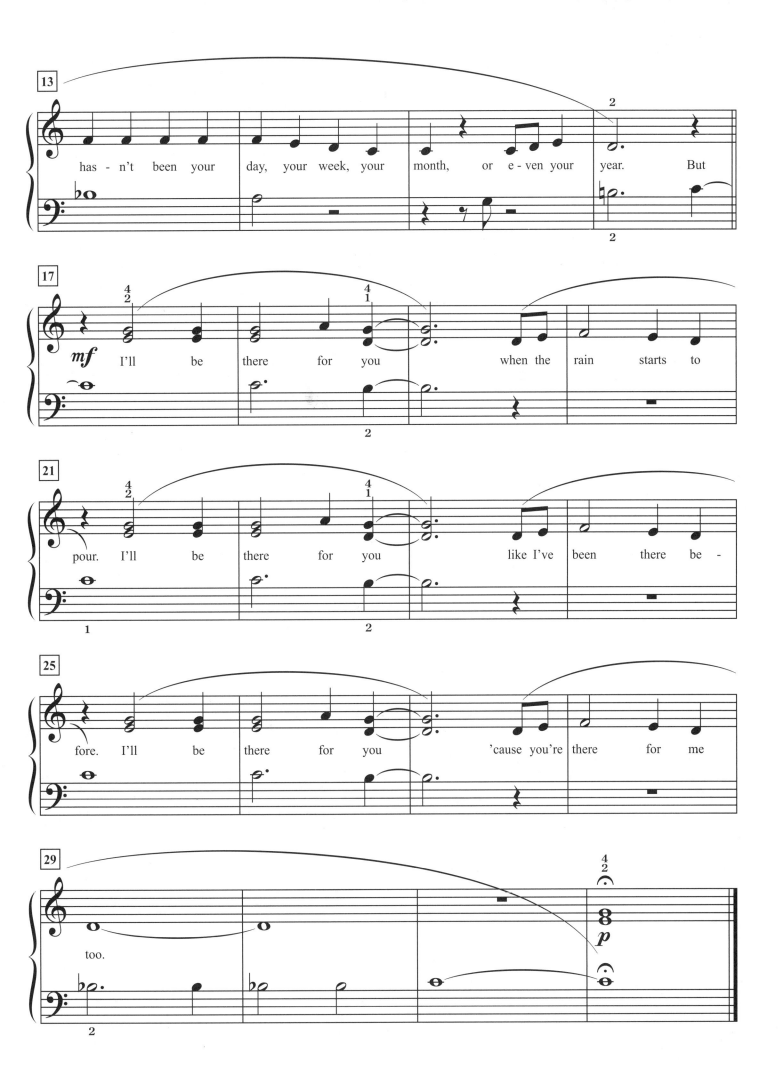

Unit Three

Recorded by the band Berlin (with lead singer Terri Nunn), "Take My Breath Away" was the first single released from the soundtrack for the 1986 film *Top Gun,* starring Tom Cruise and Kelly McGillis. The song reached #1 on the charts and won the Academy Award for Best Original Song.

TAKE MY BREATH AWAY

Music by Giorgio Moroder
Words by Tom Whitlock
Arranged by Carol Matz

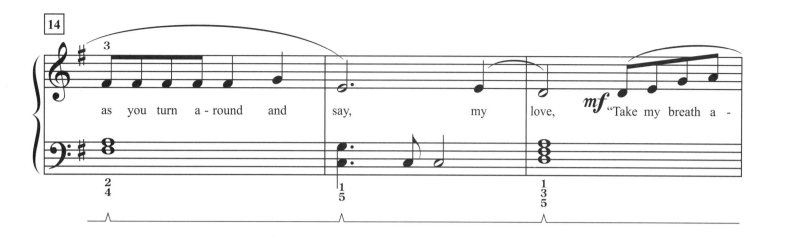

as you turn a-round and say, my love, *mf* "Take my breath a-

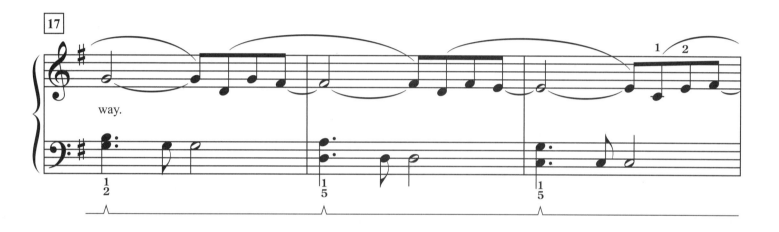

way.

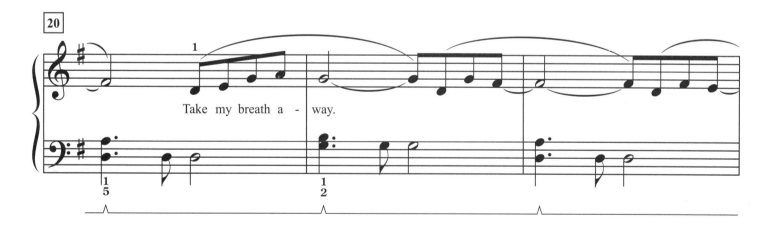

Take my breath a - way.

Take my breath a - way."

p *rit.*

Unit Four

This 1997 hit by the pop-punk band Green Day is most recognized by its subtitle, "Time of Your Life." Its reflective lyrics have made the song popular for graduation ceremonies and high school proms. The song gained further popularity when it was used in one of the last episodes of the long-running TV sitcom *Seinfeld,* during a retrospective montage of clips from the show's history.

GOOD RIDDANCE
(Time of Your Life)

Lyrics by Billie Joe
Music by Billie Joe and Green Day
Arranged by Carol Matz

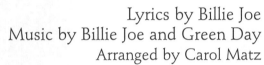

1. An - oth - er turn - ing point, a fork stuck in the road.
2. So take the pho - to - graphs and still frames in your mind.

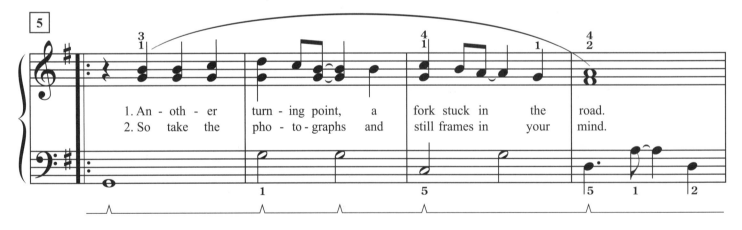

Time grabs you by the wrist, di - rects you where to go.
Hang it on a shelf in good health and good time.

Unit Five

Walt Disney's 1994 animated hit *The Lion King* won two Academy Awards: Best Original Score (by Hans Zimmer) and Best Original Song for "Can You Feel the Love Tonight," written by celebrated songwriters Elton John and Tim Rice. The song also earned Elton John a Grammy Award for Best Male Pop Vocal Performance.

CAN YOU FEEL THE LOVE TONIGHT
(from Walt Disney's *The Lion King*)

Music by Elton John
Words by Tim Rice
Arranged by Carol Matz

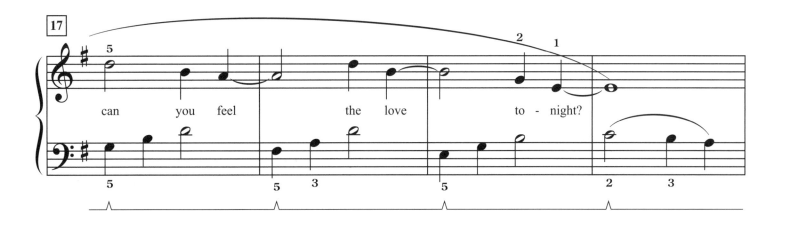

can you feel the love to - night?

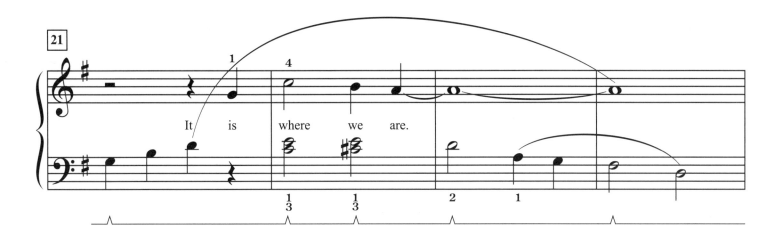

It is where we are.

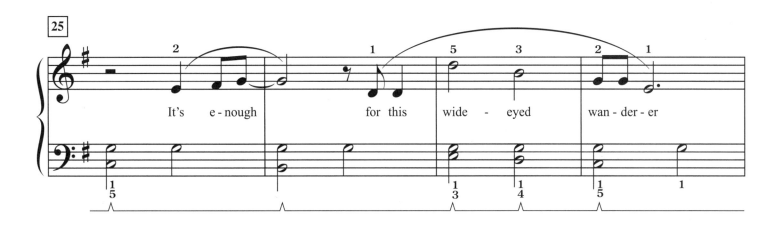

It's e - nough for this wide - eyed wan - der - er

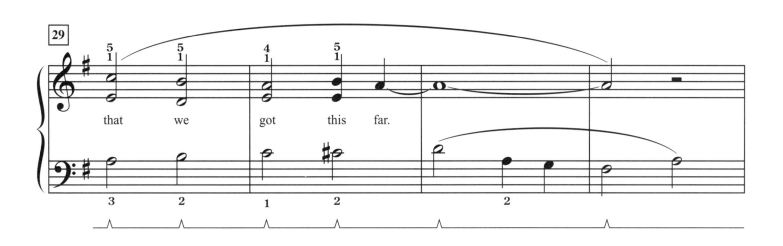

that we got this far.

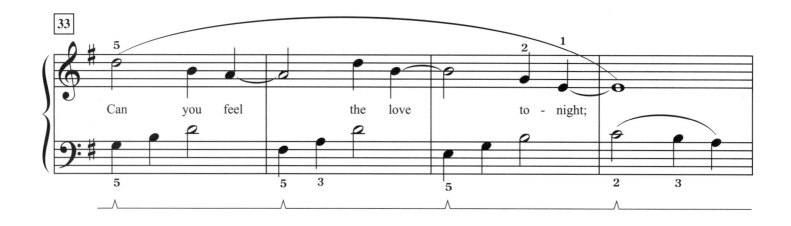

Can you feel the love to - night;

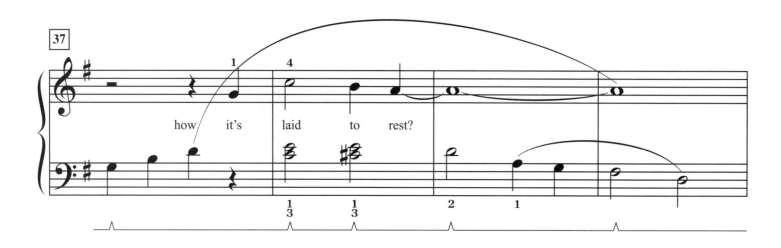

how it's laid to rest?

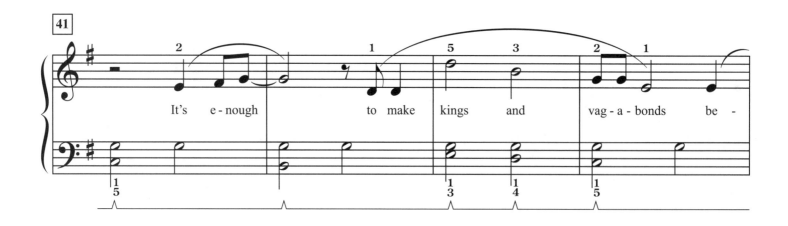

It's e - nough to make kings and vag - a - bonds be -

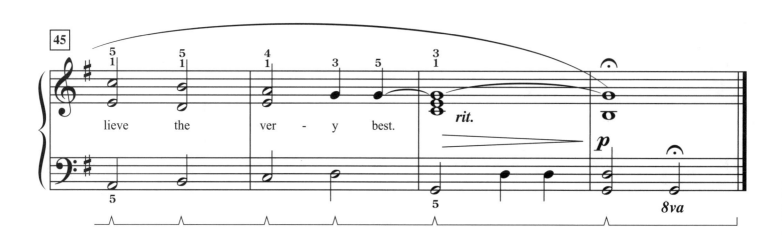

lieve the ver - y best. *rit.*

Unit Six

"Arabian Nights" is the introductory theme to the 1992 Walt Disney animated feature *Aladdin*. The film's score, composed by Alan Menken, received the Academy Award for Best Original Music Score, as well as two Golden Globe Awards. Robin Williams turned in a hilarious performance as the voice of the Genie, which earned him an MTV Movie Award for Best Comedic Performance.

ARABIAN NIGHTS
(from Walt Disney's *Aladdin*)

Words by Howard Ashman
Music by Alan Menken
Arranged by Carol Matz

Moderately

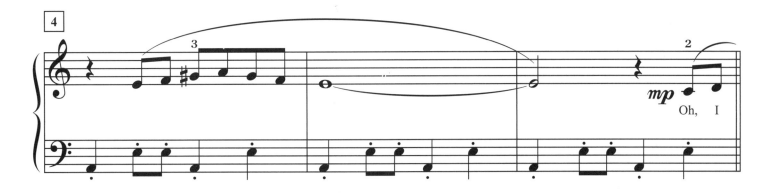

Unit Seven

Written by legendary songwriters Burt Bacharach and Carole Bayer Sager, "That's What Friends Are For" was recorded by Dionne Warwick and Friends (Gladys Knight, Elton John and Stevie Wonder) in 1985. It was originally released as a charity single benefiting the American Foundation for AIDS Research. The recording raised over three million dollars for the charity, became the #1 single of 1986, and earned two Grammy Awards.

THAT'S WHAT FRIENDS ARE FOR

Music by Burt Bacharach
Words by Carole Bayer Sager
Arranged by Carol Matz

Unit Eight

"Fame," the popular song from the 1980 musical film, was recorded by singer Irene Cara, who also played the starring role in the movie. The song won both an Academy Award and a Golden Globe for Best Original Song, and the score for *Fame* earned another Academy Award.

FAME
(from *Fame*)

Music by Michael Gore
Lyrics by Dean Pitchford
Arranged by Carol Matz

Unit Nine

"The Imperial March" is the memorable theme for *Star Wars* villain Darth Vader. Renowned film composer John Williams created this wonderfully ominous theme for the 1980 blockbuster film *Star Wars Episode V: The Empire Strikes Back.* The London Symphony Orchestra, conducted by Williams, recorded the film's score.

THE IMPERIAL MARCH
(Darth Vader's Theme)

Music by **JOHN WILLIAMS**
Arranged by Carol Matz

This beautiful song, from the 1991 Walt Disney animated film *Beauty and the Beast,* earned the Academy Award for Best Song. It was sung in the movie by award-winning singer and actress Angela Lansbury, and performed as a duet over the closing credits by well-known pop singers Céline Dion and Peabo Bryson.

BEAUTY AND THE BEAST
(from Walt Disney's *Beauty and the Beast*)

Lyrics by Howard Ashman
Music by Alan Menken
Arranged by Carol Matz

Expressively

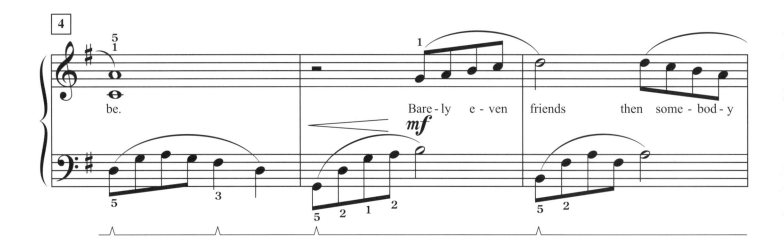

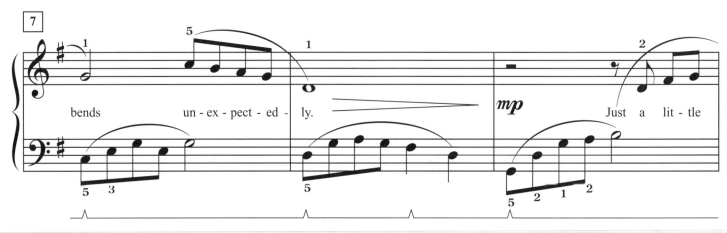

time. Tune as old as song.

Bit - ter - sweet and strange, find - ing you can change, learn - ing you were

wrong. *mp* Cer - tain as the sun

ris - ing in the east. Tale as old as time, song as old as

rhyme, Beau - ty and the Beast. *mp* *p*

rit.

8va

Unit Eleven

This #1 single by Bette Midler is from the soundtrack of the 1988 drama *Beaches,* a film in which Midler starred alongside actress Barbara Hershey. The song was named Record of the Year and Song of the Year at the Grammy Awards in 1990.

THE WIND BENEATH MY WINGS

Words and Music by
Larry Henley and Jeff Silbar
Arranged by Carol Matz

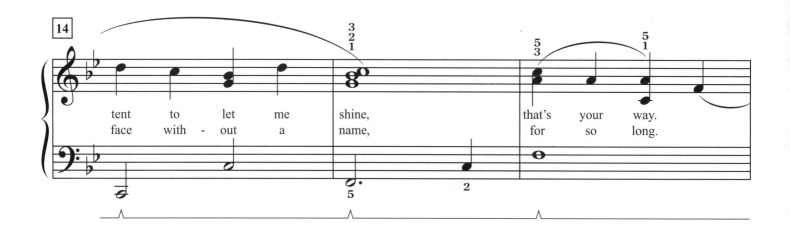

tent   to   let   me   shine,   that's   your   way.
face   with - out   a   name,   for   so   long.

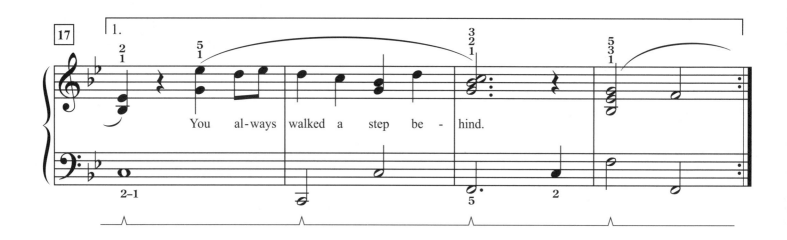

1.

You al-ways walked a step be - hind.

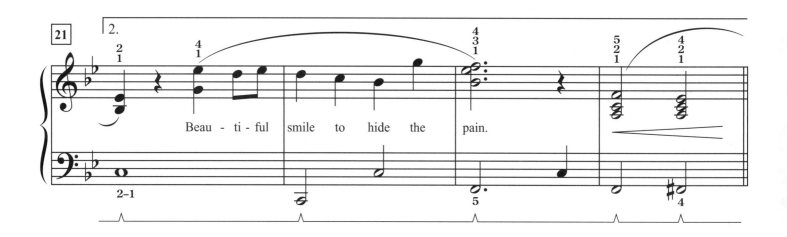

2.

Beau - ti - ful smile to hide the pain.

Did you ev - er know that you're my he - ro,

mf

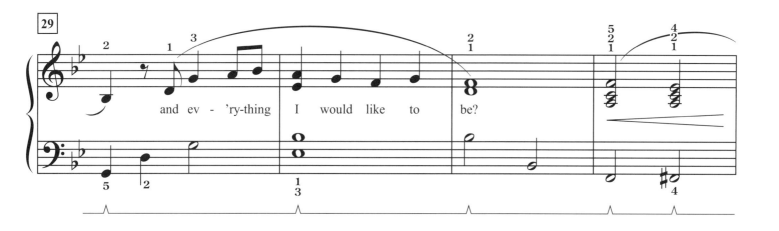

and ev - 'ry-thing   I   would   like   to   be?

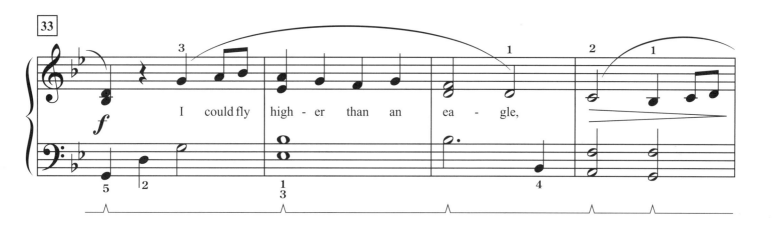

I   could fly   high - er   than   an   ea - gle,

for you   are the   wind   be - neath my   wings.

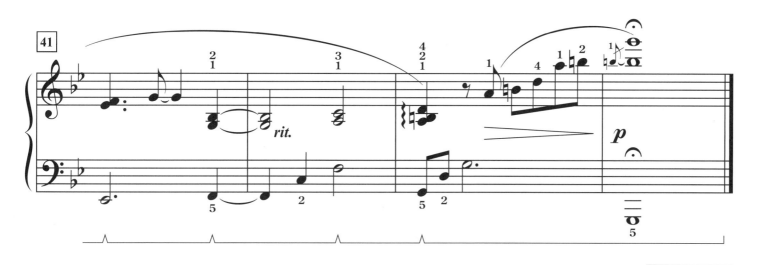

rit.

p